Investigating Household Waste Pollution

Sue Gagliardi

Wonder Books
An Imprint of The Child's World®
childsworld.com

The Child's World
childsworld.com

Published by The Child's World®
800-599-READ • www.childsworld.com

Copyright © 2023 by The Child's World®
All rights reserved. No part of this book may be reproduced or utilized in any form or by any means without written permission from the publisher.

Photography Credits
Photographs ©: iStockphoto, cover, 2, 29; Peter Gudella/Shutterstock Images, 5; Shutterstock Images, 6 (soil), 6 (paper), 6 (orange peel), 6 (plastic bottle), 11, 18, 21, 25, 27; Alexandr Bognat/Shutterstock Images, 6 (plastic bag); Egudin Ka/Shutterstock Images, 6 (soda can); Anna Hoychuk/Shutterstock Images, 9; Joaquin Corbalan P/Shutterstock Images, 12; James Stone/Shutterstock Images, 15; Sergey Mironov/Shutterstock Images, 17; Igisheva Maria/Shutterstock Images, 23; Yuriy Semak/Shutterstock Images, 31

ISBN Information
9781503858114 (Reinforced Library Binding)
9781503860087 (Portable Document Format)
9781503861442 (Online Multi-user eBook)
9781503862807 (Electronic Publication)

LCCN 2021952481

Printed in the United States of America

ABOUT THE AUTHOR

Sue Gagliardi is a teacher who writes fiction, nonfiction, and poetry for children. She is eager to explore new ways to reduce household waste pollution.

Household waste pollution can increase if people do not recycle, reuse, or throw away garbage properly.

TABLE OF CONTENTS

CHAPTER ONE

A MOUNTAIN OF GARBAGE

Eli noticed all the trash in the dumpster near his house. The dumpster was filled with food scraps, paper, and broken toys. Eli's dad told him that waste from people's homes go into landfills. These are places where garbage is buried in the ground. It can take many years for garbage to **decompose**.

Eli wanted to learn more about what happens when a lot of trash piles up. He talked to his friends, and they did some research. They found out that the trash they throw away each day is called household waste. Eli and his friends also learned that household waste causes **pollution**.

Many households produce waste that can add up to a huge amount of trash each year.

DECOMPOSING GARBAGE

PAPER	2-6 WEEKS
ORANGE PEEL	6 MONTHS
PLASTIC BAG	10-20 YEARS
SODA CAN	80-200 YEARS
PLASTIC WATER BOTTLE	450 YEARS

Garbage may decompose quickly or slowly, depending on what it is made of. In landfills, waste is sealed under a rubber and clay barrier. The barrier cuts off oxygen in the landfill. Without oxygen, the waste begins to break down. As it breaks down, the waste produces methane gas.

They discovered that animals could get sick when eating garbage from landfills. Gases from landfills pollute the air.

Eli and his friends started tracking their food waste. They were shocked at how much food they threw away in just one week. Eli realized that he grabbed a lot of food during lunch in the school cafeteria. But he ate only about half of it. He threw away the rest. He realized how wasteful he was being. If he had not taken all that food, maybe it would not have ended up in the trash.

Eli and his friends wanted to do something to reduce waste. They did not want their trash to pile up and cause pollution.

PLASTIC TRASH

Discarded plastic items can end up in waterways such as rivers and oceans. Marine animals can get sick from eating the plastic. Birds and other animals can be harmed when they eat plastics. The plastics can cause a blockage in their stomachs. This can cause them to become sick or starve.

They found a way to help with their food waste problem. They learned that a lot of food scraps can be **composted**. The compost can be put into garden soil. That helps make plants grow. Eli made a list of the food items he could compost. He learned that fruits, vegetables, and nut shells could be used. He was also surprised to learn that grass clippings, leaves, straw, and even his dog's fur could be composted, too.

Eli and his friends made a Composting Club at school. Their club helped spread the word about reducing food waste. They told their classmates about composting. They talked to their teachers and the principal. Soon, their club had a composting bin in the cafeteria. There was a big sign above the bin telling people what they could compost. At lunch, students began tossing their food scraps into the compost bin instead of the trash.

Composting food makes soil richer, which helps plants grow healthier.

Eli and his friends were proud that their Composting Club was helping reduce food waste.

Household waste comes from many things. It includes plastic, paper, glass, and metal. Household waste also includes food and yard waste. Many households also throw away **hazardous** and electronic waste. A lot of this trash ends up in landfills. Animal homes are destroyed when an area of land is cleared to make a landfill. The United States has more than 3,000 active landfills. The average size of a landfill is 600 acres (243 ha). These landfills have destroyed 1.8 million acres (728,434 ha) of animal habitat.

Landfills can be harmful to people, too. Gas is released from the waste as it breaks down. These gases can produce air pollution. Also, harmful chemicals may leak out of landfills. They get into the water supply. These chemicals can make drinking water unsafe for people and animals.

CHAPTER TWO

FOOD WASTE

Most households throw away a lot of food each year. In the United States, each person throws out around 23 pounds (10 kg) of good food each month. This means that households may be throwing out around $1,800 worth of food per month. Many hungry people could have been fed with this food.

Instead of throwing away leftovers after a meal, people can save the food for future meals or compost it.

If people buy only the food they need, they can help reduce food waste in landfills.

There are many causes of food waste. People can buy too much food at the grocery store. Some of them might buy more food if they are hungry. Others go to the store without a plan or a list of things to buy. All that extra food can end up rotten and uneaten in the fridge or pantry.

Another cause for food waste is that people can store food in the wrong place. After coming back from the grocery store, raw meat, dairy products, and salads need to go into the refrigerator. This is because these foods can spoil very easily. And rotten food eventually ends up in the garbage.

Food that is thrown away will go to landfills. In the United States, food waste is the largest form of landfill waste. This adds to the pollution problem. **Bacteria** from food waste can get into the soil. The bacteria can harm plants and animals. It can enter the water stream and harm marine animals. Rotting food scraps that are not thrown away correctly can make birds, dogs, and other animals sick when they eat them. As the food begins to rot, it attracts ticks and mites. These insects can attach to birds and other animals. They can carry diseases that make birds and other animals sick.

Discarded liquids and oils can stick to birds' wings. This can make it difficult for birds to fly. Birds can also get sick when they try to clean the oil off with their beaks. Water pollution from food waste can make drinking water unsafe for people, too.

The breakdown of food waste in landfills can cause other environmental problems. For example, rotting food waste releases harmful gases such as methane. Methane traps heat on Earth. It is known as a greenhouse gas. Over time, different human activities have created more greenhouse gases. These have made Earth warmer. When the Earth warms, glaciers melt. This then causes sea levels to rise.

WASTING FOOD

About one-third of food in the United States is wasted every year. The total food waste is around 1.3 billion tons (1.3 trillion kg) of food. The wasted food costs about $1 trillion to make. This is enough to feed more than three billion people.

Animals such as polar bears are affected by climate change. Melting glaciers make it harder for polar bears to find food.

Greenhouse gases such as methane contribute to **climate change**. Climate change impacts Earth's weather. Over time, storms may get more dangerous. Also, there may be less rainfall, which can lead to the land drying up. Many types of animals might disappear because of climate change. Methane from food waste adds to this problem.

CHAPTER THREE

HAZARDOUS AND ELECTRONIC WASTE

Hazardous and electronic waste are two more types of household waste pollution. Some hazardous waste includes cleaning products such as furniture polish or drain cleaner. These products have dangerous chemicals. If the chemicals get into the environment, they can pollute the water and soil. This can harm animals and plants, which need healthy soil and water to survive. It can also make drinking water unsafe for people. Household hazardous waste must be disposed of in safe ways. For example, many cities and towns have hazardous waste drop-off locations or collections.

Cleaning products have a lot of chemicals in them. It is not good for these chemicals to get into the environment.

Used electronics can be recycled at community drop-off locations. They can also be recycled in many electronics stores.

People can also contribute to electronic waste. Electronic waste happens when people throw old electronics into the trash. When electronics are thrown in the trash, they end up in landfills. However, in some states, like Wisconsin and California, it is illegal to put electronic waste in landfills. People must use e-waste recycling programs instead.

Electronic waste can include TVs, printers, lamps, phones, and microwaves. These electronics may be made with heavy metals such as copper or lead. If people do not throw electronics away correctly, these metals can get back into the soil, water, and air. In large amounts, these metals are hurtful to people and animals. They can damage organs. They may even cause cancer. In hot weather, electronic waste is especially harmful. The heat causes dangerous chemicals to be released into the air. This causes air pollution and poses serious health risks.

In addition, people sometimes burn electronic waste. This also contributes to air pollution.

Some cities or companies have programs to collect electronic waste. They can recycle the electronics carefully so they do not cause pollution. It is important for people to practice safe recycling of electronic waste. Improper recycling can harm people, animals, and the environment. The United States exports electronic waste to other countries, including China and India. These countries might not have safe practices in place.

E-WASTE RECYCLING

Many stores offer electronics recycling services. For example, Best Buy offers free recycling for electronics such as phones, cameras, and cables. Also, Apple offers free recycling for cell phones and other Apple products. People can even trade their Apple devices for credit. They can use their credit for a discount on future purchases.

Without safety **precautions**, electronic waste can release dangerous toxins into the environment.

In 2019, the United States had 59 million tons (53 billion kg) of electronic waste. This waste included cell phones and computers. The waste weighed as much as 350 ocean liners. A lot of people discard older cell phones or other devices. In many cases, the old devices could be recycled or reused. Some communities may have recycling programs for electronics. They use the parts to make new devices.

People can donate their used but working electronics to thrift stores.

CHAPTER FOUR

FINDING SOLUTIONS

Household waste pollution is a growing problem in the United States and in countries around the world. It does not only affect the environment. Household waste can have a long-lasting impact on humans and animals. But the good news is that people can do many things to cut down on this pollution.

Food waste can be reduced when people buy only the food they need. But if a person buys too much food, he or she can donate it to food banks. These places give food to hungry people who do not have money to buy food.

Also, people can reduce waste by purchasing fresh fruits and vegetables without packaging. Less packaging helps to reduce the amount of plastic waste.

Taking a reusable bag to grocery stores can help reduce plastic or paper waste.

Growing vegetables in containers or in a garden can help reduce household waste. People can compost fruit and vegetable scraps. Eggshells, coffee grounds, plants, and tea bags can also be used to make compost. The compost can then be placed in the soil to help plants grow.

People can reduce their use of single-use plastics. These plastics include water bottles and plastic utensils that people use only one time and then throw away. One way to stop using single-use plastics is by drinking from reusable bottles.

HABITAT FOR HUMANITY

Habitat for Humanity is an organization that builds homes for people in need. To help their mission, they have stores called Habitat ReStores. Their stores sell donated furniture, household items, and building materials. When people buy from resell stores, this helps keep waste out of landfills. People can also donate their used items. The donated items are sold to people in the community who really need them.

Donating is one way to recycle used items. Clothes, old toys, kitchenware, and furniture can help people who are in need.

People can also donate items they no longer need instead of throwing them away. They can find other ways to reuse these items to help reduce household waste. Many thrift stores accept used items such as clothing, books, toys, and other household objects.

Many communities have recycling programs. People can place certain items in bins for community recycling. If a neighborhood does not have a recycling program, people can contact the city. They can ask about starting a recycling program.

Also, some states have a "bottle bill." People can take their used soda cans, plastic water bottles, and glass bottles to recycling centers for money. Generally, each bottle earns 5 to 10 cents. This can add up if people collect their used bottles each month.

People can reduce their use of household hazardous products. One way to do this is by making natural cleaning products. These products have safe ingredients, like baking soda or white vinegar, that do not cause pollution. Local cities can also give information about how to handle household hazardous waste disposal.

Helping reduce household waste can be very simple. It can start with throwing away waste in the proper bins.

Household waste can contribute to pollution in many ways. But people can help reduce pollution by recycling and reusing materials instead of throwing them away. People can learn about disposing of hazardous materials in safe ways. When people reduce their household waste, they help living things and the environment.

FAST FACTS

- A lot of household waste goes to landfills. It can cause pollution that harms living things.
- Household food waste is a growing problem around the world. Some people compost their food scraps so they do not end up in landfills.
- In landfills, chemicals from food waste can leak into the soil. These chemicals can harm plants and animals. In addition, food waste in landfills releases harmful gases such as methane. Methane contributes to climate change.
- Many household cleaning products have harmful chemicals. These products can leak toxins into the soil and water.
- Electronic waste can contain lead and other harmful materials.
- To decrease household waste, people can make sure to buy only the food they will actually eat. People can reduce how many single-use plastics they use. They can make sure to recycle objects in a safe way.

MAKE YOUR OWN COMPOSTER

MATERIALS

- An empty 2-liter soda bottle
- A tray
- Dirt
- Water
- Leftover food such as fruits, vegetables, and eggshells
- Yard waste

DIRECTIONS

1. Ask an adult to help you poke holes in the bottom of the bottle. Then cut off the top of the bottle.
2. Add dirt to cover the bottom of the bottle, and add yard waste such as hay, straw, and leaves. After every meal, add pieces of leftover fruits, vegetables, or eggshells.
3. Pour water into the bottle whenever the contents look dry. Make sure the bottle is on a tray so leaking water does not make a mess.
4. See what happens to the contents over time. How do they change?
5. When everything has decomposed, add your compost to garden soil.

GLOSSARY

bacteria (bak-TEER-ee-uh) Bacteria are small organisms that can be seen only with a microscope. Some bacteria are harmful and can cause sickness.

climate change (KLY-mit CHAYNJ) Climate change refers to long-term changes in global temperatures. Food waste in landfills can contribute to climate change.

composted (KOM-pohst-ud) If something is composted, this means it has decomposed and been turned into healthy soil. Leaves, grasses, and fruit and vegetable scraps can be composted.

decompose (dee-kum-POHZ) Decompose means to break down or rot. It takes many years for landfill waste to decompose.

hazardous (HAZ-ur-duhs) Something that is hazardous is dangerous. Household cleaning products can be hazardous to the environment.

pollution (puh-LOO-shuhn) Pollution is something harmful that gets into the air, land, or water. Household waste can cause air and water pollution.

precautions (pri-KAW-shuns) Precautions are steps taken to prevent something harmful from happening. People should take precautions when disposing of hazardous waste.

WAYS YOU CAN HELP

- Reduce food waste and compost food scraps.
- Reuse items or donate items you no longer need.
- Buy items with minimal packaging to reduce waste.
- Reduce single-use plastics.
- Drink from reusable water bottles instead of plastic ones.

FIND OUT MORE

In the Library

French, Jess. *What a Waste*.
New York, NY: DK Publishing, 2019.

Greenfield, Rob. *Zero Waste Kids*.
Beverly, MA: Quarry Books, 2022.

Minoglio, Andrea. *Our World Out of Balance*.
San Francisco, CA: Blue Dot Kids Press, 2021.

On the Web

Visit our website for links about investigating household waste pollution: **childsworld.com/links**

Note to Parents, Teachers, and Librarians: We routinely verify our Web links to make sure they are safe and active sites. So encourage your readers to check them out!

INDEX